THE WOW AND THE HOW

ROBOTS AND AI

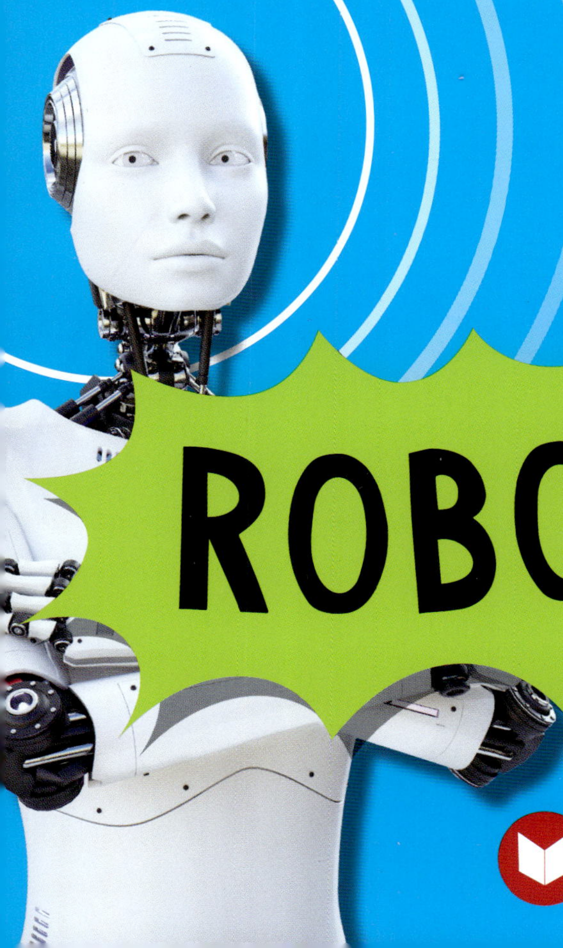

LIZ LENNON

Gareth Stevens PUBLISHING

Please visit our website, www.garethstevens.com. For a free color catalog of all our high-quality books, call toll free 1-800-542-2595 or fax 1-877-542-2596.

Cataloging-in-Publication Data
Names: Lennon, Liz.
Title: Robots and AI / Liz Lennon.
Description: Buffalo, NY : Gareth Stevens Publishing, 2026. | Series: The wow and the how | Includes glossary and index.
Identifiers: ISBN 9781482473124 (pbk.) | ISBN 9781482473131 (library bound) | ISBN 9781482473148 (ebook)
Subjects: LCSH: Robots--Juvenile literature. | Artificial intelligence--Juvenile literature.
Classification: LCC TJ211.2 L466 2026 | DDC 629.892--dc23

Published in 2026 by
Gareth Stevens Publishing
2544 Clinton St.
Buffalo, NY 14224

First published in Great Britain in 2024 by Hodder & Stoughton

Authors: Paul Rockett, Victoria Brooker, Sarah Peutrill, Julia Bird, Grace Glendinning, Elise Short, Melanie Palmer

Series designer: Rocket Design (East Anglia) Ltd

Picture credits:
Georgia Institute of Technology: 28.
NASA/JPL-Caltech/MSSS: 21b.
Science Photo Library: Benny J 15b.
Shutterstock: AlsuSh 10; Anatolir 8b; Archy13 4-5bg; bercheck 8-9bg; Bookzv 17c; Bsd studio 25c; comsorg 27c; Corona Borealis Studio 4tl, 4tr, 4cl, 12-13;Diversepixel 18-19bg; Favebrush 9b; Frame Art 11ca; fukume/Elements furnished by NASA 17b; Furita 15c; Gargantiopa 16cl; Gearstd 5tr, 25b; GrandeDuc 24; Higyou 14c; Sarah Holmlund front cover l, 1l; Rosa Jay 29; Ilya Kalinin 7b; Will Hilton-Kent 19b; Koya979 front cover r, 1r; Josh McCann 23; Mirror Image Studio 16-17bg; Joseph Moawad 26-27bg; Dean Murray 26c; Ostariyanov 4-5b; Alexander_P 27b; Vitalii Petrenko 13b; shop_py 16cl, 16cr; Stockakia 18c; Sudowoodo 21c; Sunward Art 14bg; Andrey Suslov 4cb, 6, 7c, 22bl; Syverarts Vector 22br; Triff/Elements furnished by NASA 20; Azal Valeev 8cr; Vectorpocket 8cl; Victor Zastolskiy 22-23bg; ZeinousGDS 5bc.
Wikimedia: Christies 11c.

All additional design elements from Shutterstock or drawn by designer.

Printed in the United States of America

CPSIA compliance information: Batch #CSGS26: For further information contact Gareth Stevens at 1-800-542-2595.

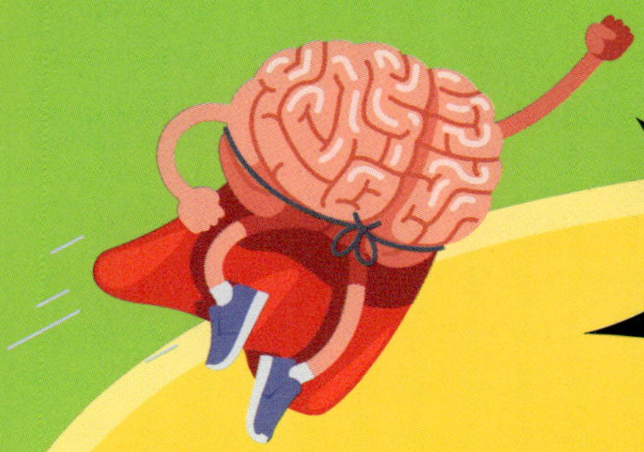

CONTENTS

The WOW of robots and AI! → **4**

Robots use AI to self-repair! → **6**

Supercomputers work out millions of chess moves a second! → **8**

AI can create ANY picture in just seconds! → **10**

Nanobots can cure diseases! → **12**

Robots can poop! → **14**

Robots shoot lasers to find their way! → **16**

Ice robots will build (and repair) themselves! → **18**

Robots can do experiments on Mars! → **20**

Robot snakes can save lives! → **22**

You can be half human, half robot! → **24**

The first robot was invented over 2,000 years ago! → **26**

A robot sloth is the latest eco hero! → **28**

Glossary → **30**

Further reading → **31**

Index → **32**

THE WOW OF ROBOTS AND AI!

Robots are AMAZING! Robots can save lives, repair themselves, and even do experiments on Mars! WOW!

A robot works because of **HOW** it is programmed. Robots are often controlled by AI (Artificial Intelligence). AI is when a computer or robot can learn, understand and make decisions. The robot uses this information to perform tasks without human help.

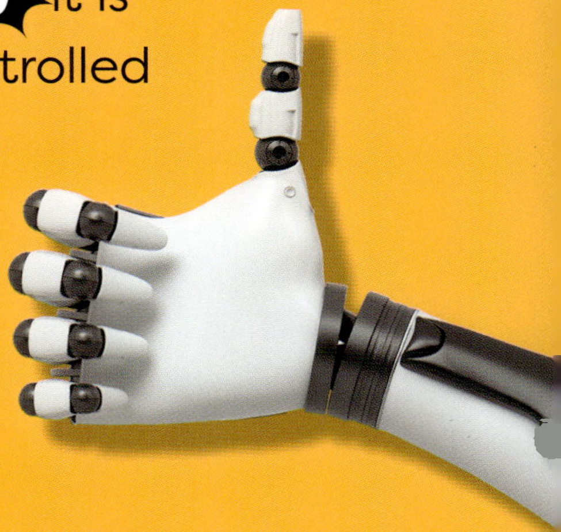

Robots are helping humans in so many ways. From art, medicine, and the environment to transportation, technology, and even sports, robots can be found in many of our daily lives. Can you think of any robots in your home?

Discover amazing facts about robots including some that may challenge what you thought you knew. Find out the science behind these to understand more about how different robots work. Can you find out more **WOW** facts about robots and AI?

WOW!

Robots use AI to self-repair!

THEY CAN LOCATE AN INJURY AND THEN HEAL THEMSELVES.

HOW?

New AI-enabled sensor nodes allow robots to detect and deal with any malfunction. These brain-like electronic devices act as artificial pain receptors, just like in a human brain.

After finding any damage, such as a cut or break, a robot uses a self-healing ion gel contained within its outer layer. The molecules in this gel begin to interact, meaning the robot can heal the damage by itself, without human help.

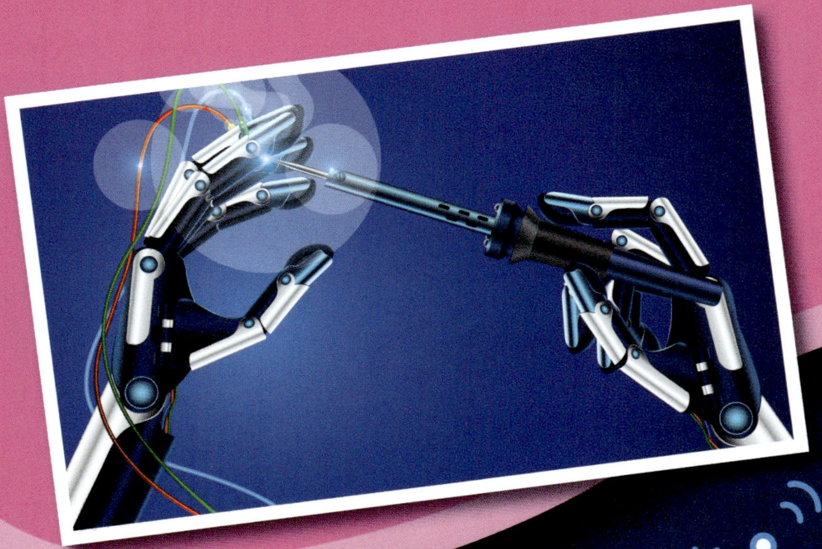

AMAZING ROBOTS

Some robots that damage their legs can find a new way of walking or moving in under 2 minutes!

WOW!
Supercomputers work out millions of chess moves a second!
DEEP BLUE WAS A FAMOUS COMPUTER THAT USED AI TO WORK OUT THE BEST MOVES IN CHESS.
Can you play chess as fast as me?
No, but I can fix you when you break down!

HOW?

Deep Blue first beat a human world chess champion in 1997. It did this by working at superfast speed using complex algorithms and parallel processing.

An algorithm is a set of instructions that tell a computer what to do, step by step. Parallel processing is when a computer divides a task into smaller parts and works on them at the same time, to complete the task faster. It's like having many people work on different parts of a puzzle at the same time.

AMAZING ROBOTS

Deep Blue was made to play chess, but it helped developers learn to design a computer to tackle other complicated problems, including discovering new medicines.

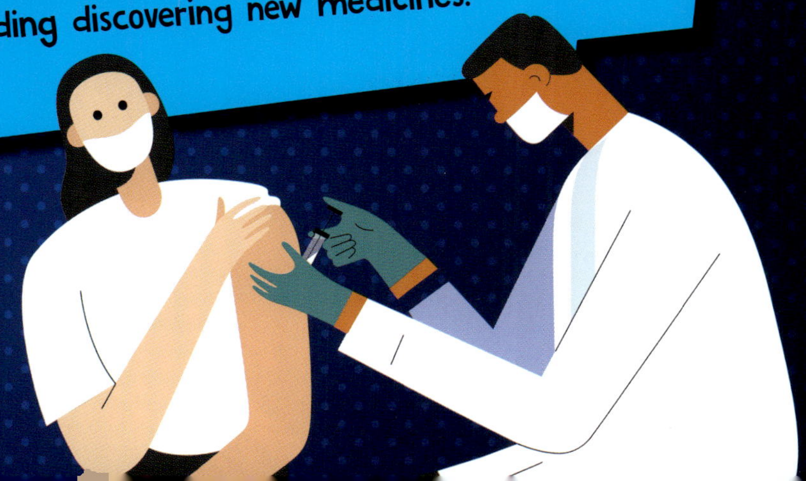

WOW!

AI can create ANY picture in just seconds!

THINK OF THE CRAZIEST IMAGE YOU CAN. AI CAN MAKE IT HAPPEN IN THE BLINK OF AN EYE!

HOW?

AI art programs are trained to recognize millions of different objects and to memorize key information about them.

When you type a description of the new picture you want to create into the program, AI speedily scans through its memory bank of images. You might type "a cat playing a guitar in space." The program identifies the key words "cat," "guitar," and "space" and puts them together to create a new picture that is totally unique.

AMAZING ROBOTS

This AI-created artwork sold for $432,000 in 2018!

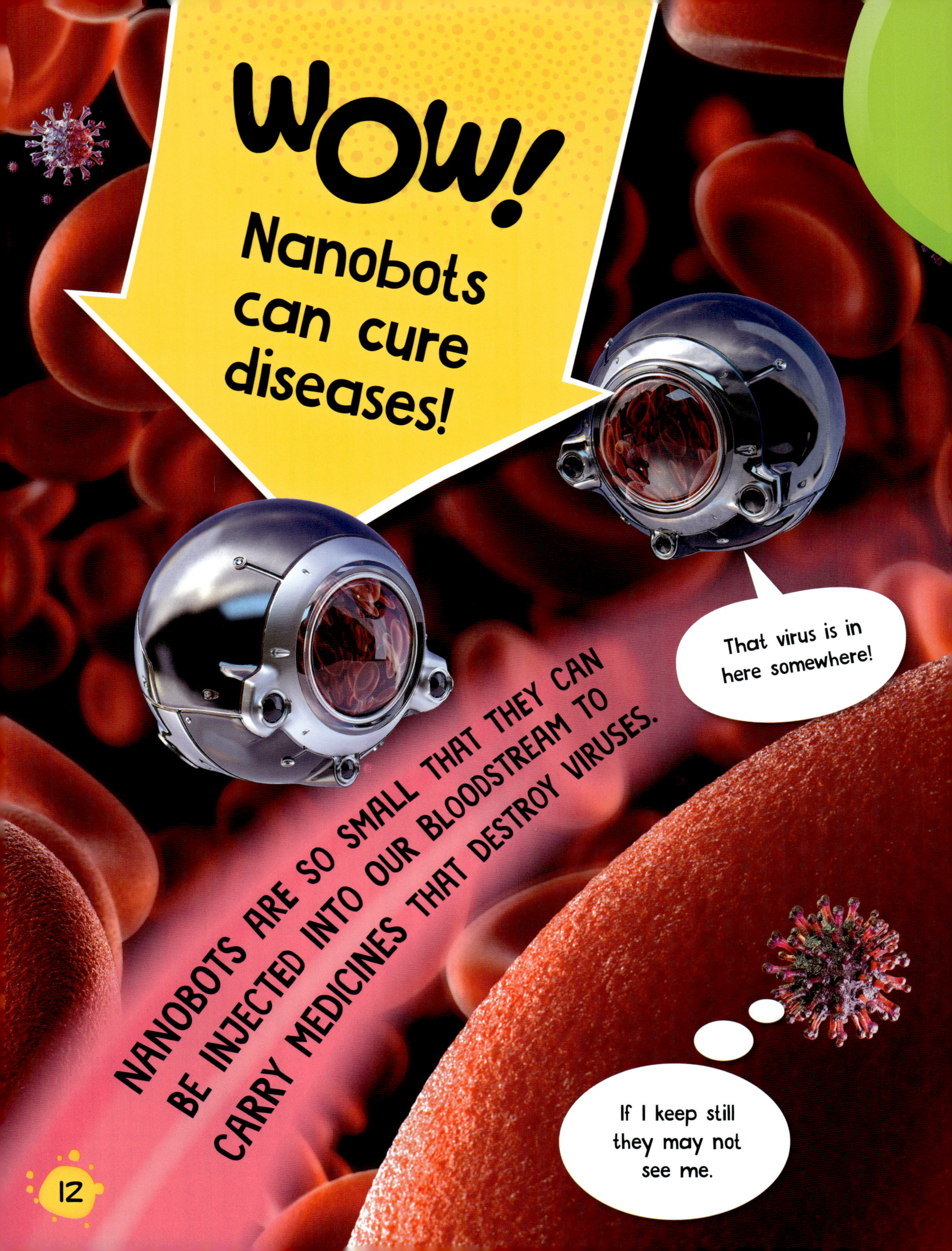

WOW!

Nanobots can cure diseases!

NANOBOTS ARE SO SMALL THAT THEY CAN BE INJECTED INTO OUR BLOODSTREAM TO CARRY MEDICINES THAT DESTROY VIRUSES.

That virus is in here somewhere!

If I keep still they may not see me.

HOW?

Nanobots are robots so small you can't see them. These tiny machines are measured in nanometers (1 millimeter = 1,000,000 nanometers). They can be made from different materials, such as metals, plastics, or even DNA. Some move around the body on their own and others are controlled from the outside of the body using magnets.

Nanobots are given instructions to do specific tasks in the body via radio signals. They can also communicate with each other and work together to carry out more difficult jobs, such as unclogging a blood vessel to prevent a heart attack.

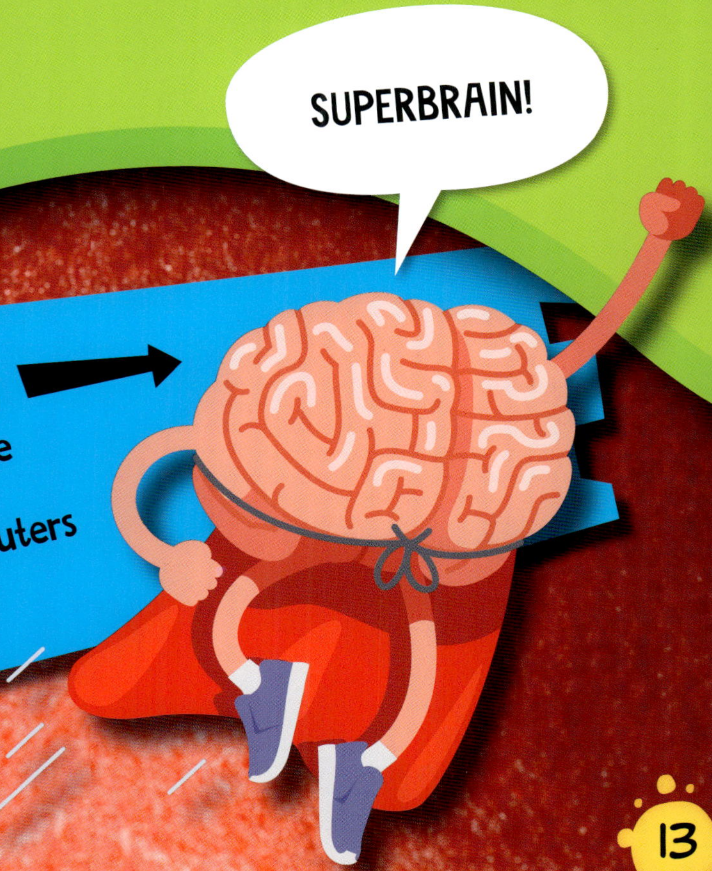

AMAZING ROBOTS

Scientists are exploring how to make nanobots connect to our brains. This would enable us to control computers and machines just by thinking.

WOW! Robots can poop!

SOME ROBOTS, KNOWN AS ECOBOTS, CAN EJECT THEIR OWN WASTE.

HOW?

EcoBot III is a little robot that helps to keep our environment clean. It eats "food" such as leaves, dirt, and poop. Just like when we eat food and our body produces waste that needs to come out, EcoBot III also has waste that it needs to get rid of.

Inside EcoBot III, there is a special part called the "waste chamber." When EcoBot III senses that its waste chamber is full, it uses a system of pumps and motors to push the waste out. Once every 24 hours, the waste is pushed through a pump into a litter box.

AMAZING ROBOTS

Instead of using batteries or electricity like most robots, EcoBot III is powered by bacteria!

WOW!

Robots shoot lasers to find their way!

ROBOTS CAN SENSE DISTANCES BY SHOOTING OUT LASER BEAMS.

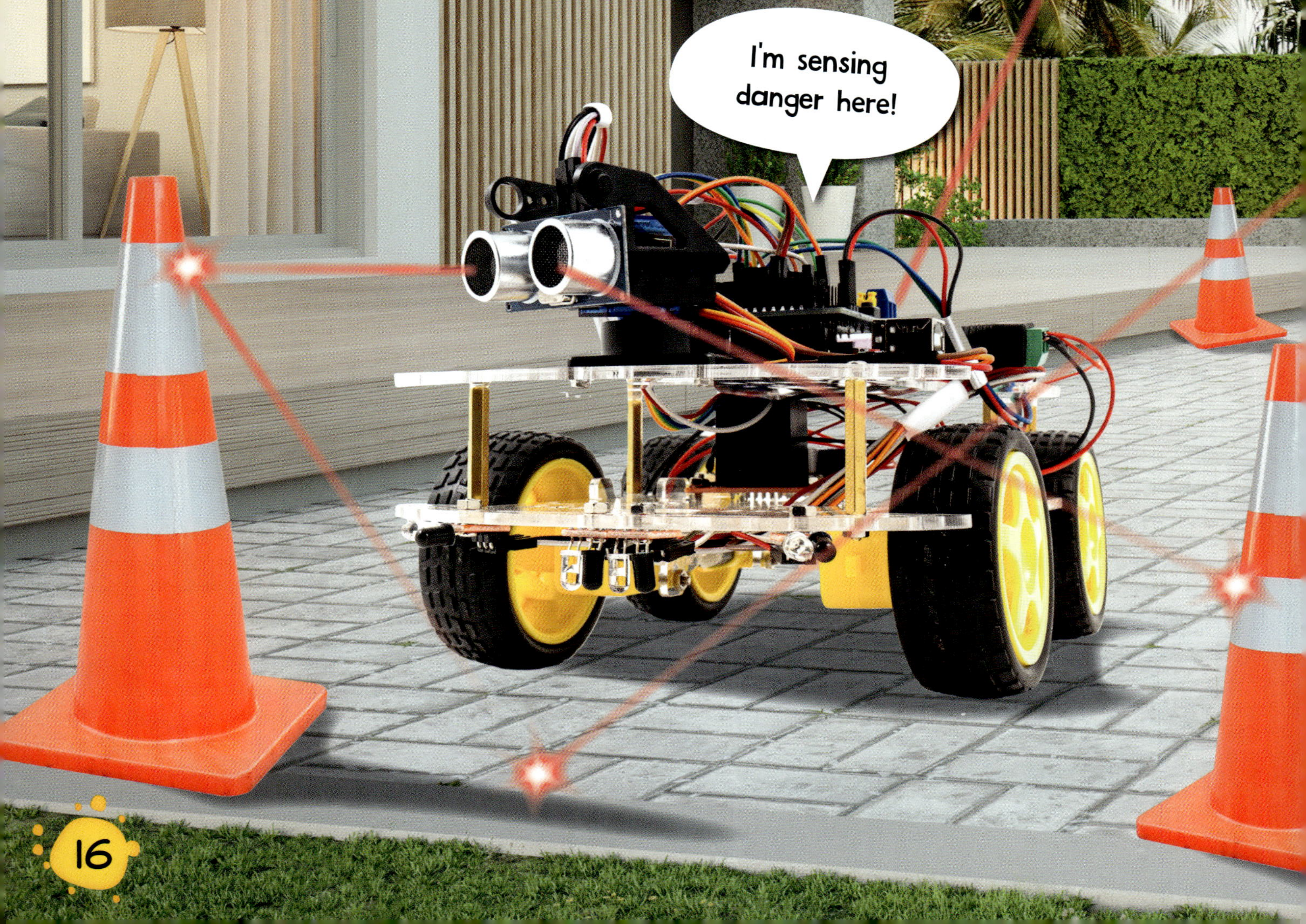

LiDAR (short for Light Detection And Ranging) is a type of sensor that helps a robot make sense of its surroundings. LiDAR measures how long it takes laser beams to bounce back from obstacles, such as walls and furniture. It also assesses how strong the beams are when they return. The longer it takes the laser beam to return to the sensor, the further away the object is.

All this information is put together to create a detailed map of where the robot is so it can plan its route and avoid obstacles.

AMAZING ROBOTS

Because LiDAR is so effective, many different types of robot use it to find their way, from self-driving cars and rovers on Mars to vacuum-cleaning robots and factory robots.

WOW!

Ice robots will build (and repair) themselves!

SCIENTISTS HAVE TO INVENT EXTREME ROBOTS TO EXPLORE EXTREME ENVIRONMENTS!

HOW?

Exploring harsh ice caps and frozen worlds in the far reaches of our solar system would be no problem for a robot made of ice! Engineers have designed a robot concept that would use the ice in these dangerous environments to keep itself moving and exploring.

Scientists would send the bot's main computer base to the location and activate it. Powered by solar power, the idea is that the bot would construct moving parts for itself out of ice. It would also set up a repair station (in case it loses a wheel or melts a bit as it works).

With solar power and ice parts working together, an ice bot could keep going for a long time on a freezing planet!

AMAZING ROBOTS

There are already submarine bots under the ice in Antarctica. These are getting ready to explore Jupiter's super-icy moon, Europa.

Europa is covered by a thick ice layer, over a huge ocean.

WOW! Robots can do experiments on Mars!

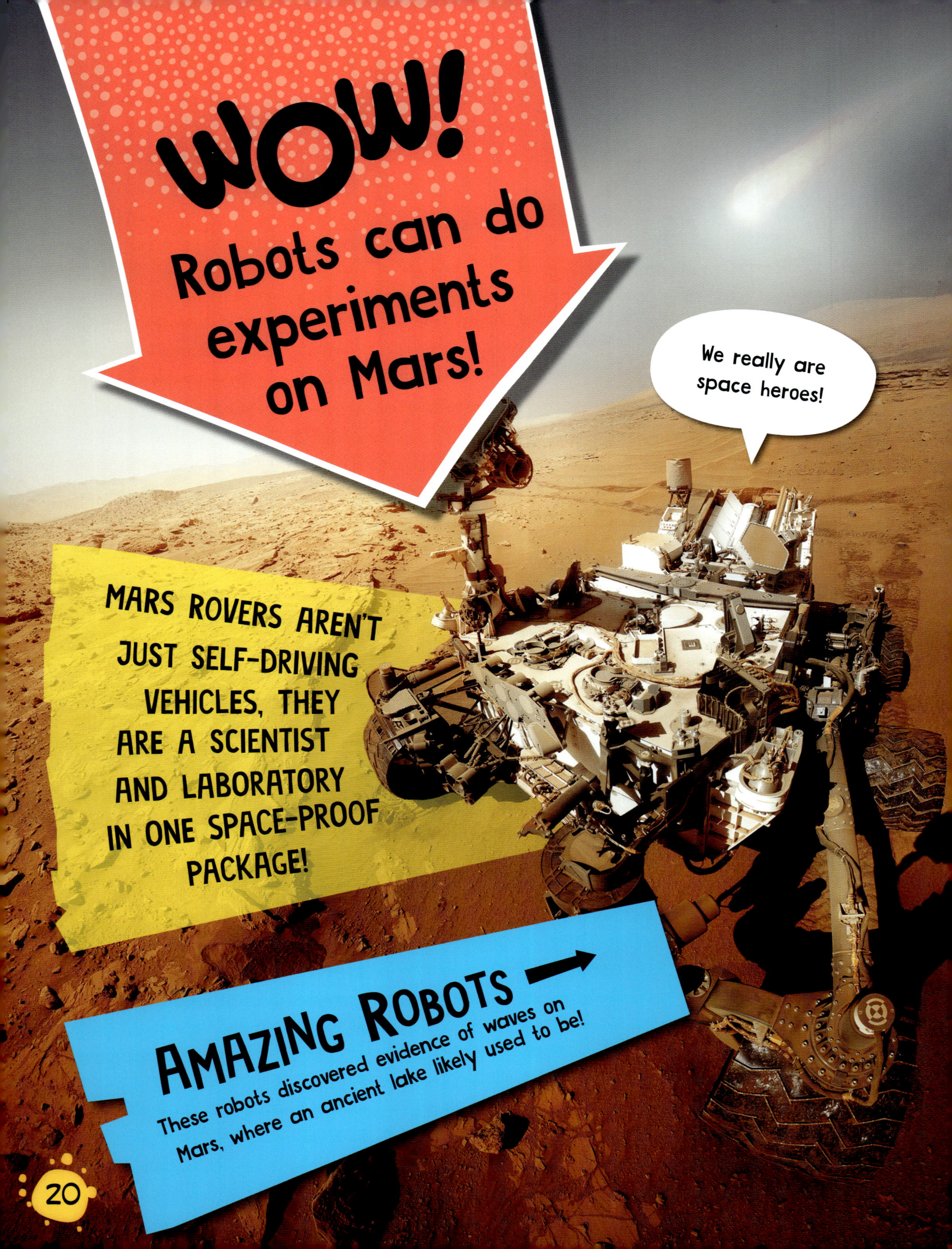

MARS ROVERS AREN'T JUST SELF-DRIVING VEHICLES, THEY ARE A SCIENTIST AND LABORATORY IN ONE SPACE-PROOF PACKAGE!

AMAZING ROBOTS →

These robots discovered evidence of waves on Mars, where an ancient lake likely used to be!

HOW?

Mars rovers act like robotic scientists. These robots use their arms, drills, and scoops to investigate the outside and inside of Martian rocks, as well as take samples of the soil on Mars' surface.

Inside the rover is a laboratory, which can analyze soil samples. Some have lasers that can vaporize bits of Martian rock up to 23 feet (7 m) away, and can identify what elements the rock is made from.

The Mars robot, Perseverance, has mirrors to help with some tests.

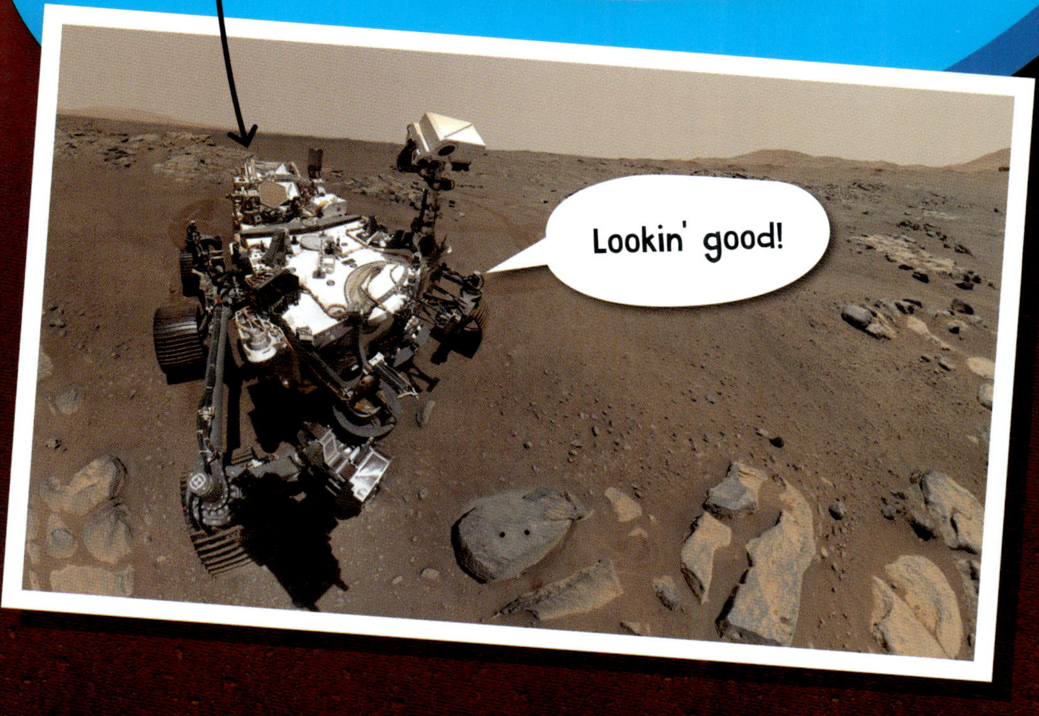

WOW!

Robot snakes can save lives!

ROBOT SNAKES ARE USED TO FIND PEOPLE TRAPPED IN COLLAPSED BUILDINGS OR OTHER DANGEROUS SPACES.

HOW?

Snake robots are a type of robot that mimics the movement of real snakes. They're made of a series of connected sections that form a flexible body that can move and twist like a snake.

The size and shape of a snake robot means that they can move through tight spaces, such as pipes or rubble, where wheeled or legged robots cannot go. They are ideal for disaster relief, where they can help to locate people who need rescuing.

AMAZING ROBOTS

Nature has inspired lots of robot designs, including robotic birds, bats, insects, and even spiders.

WOW!

You can be half human, half robot!

CYBORGS ARE REAL!

How?

In books and movies, a cyborg is a robot that is part human and part machine. In real life, a cyborg can also mean someone whose body has had a mechanical or electronic device added to it. In 1998, Kevin Warwick, a university professor, had a microchip put under his skin. From this, Kevin was able to operate devices such as room lights, door locks, and elevators.

Kevin had another chip put into his nervous system, the system of nerves that control a body. He was able to control another robot's hands without touching them.

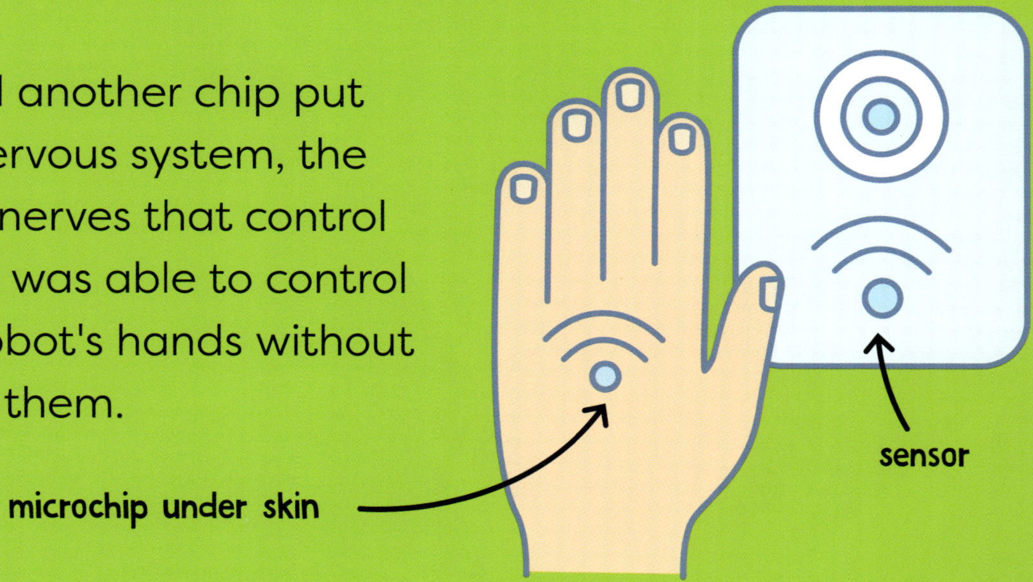

Amazing Robots

Brain-computer interfaces connect the brain to a robotic system, which has helped people to control prosthetic limbs with their thoughts!

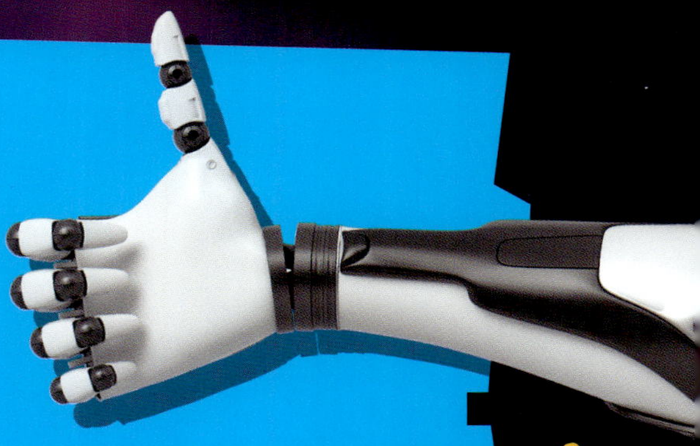

WOW!

The first robot was invented over 2,000 years ago!

ONE OF THE FIRST KNOWN ROBOTS WAS A FLYING PIGEON!

HOW?

The ancient Greek philosopher, Archytas, was said to have designed and built the first flying device, a steam-powered pigeon. The bird sat on a water boiler and, once its body was filled with enough steam, it flew off the boiler and into the air. It is believed that this bird could fly for 650 feet (200 m)!

WHOOSH!

AMAZING ROBOTS

The "Digesting Duck" was an early robot created in the 18th century. It could flap its wings, drink water, eat food, and even poop!

WOW!

A robot sloth is the latest eco hero!

THE SLOTHBOT IS HELPING US TO LEARN MORE ABOUT CLIMATE CHANGE.

Just hanging out, being eco-awesome!

HOW?

Inspired by real-life sloths, this cute robot proves it's okay to take things slow and steady. It hangs on a cable strung high in the trees for weeks or months at a time. While there, its sensors collect valuable information on temperature, weather patterns, and carbon dioxide levels. Scientists can use this data to see how conditions are changing in forests over time.

Just like a real sloth, SlothBot is very energy-efficient and spends a lot of time resting. When its battery runs low, it creeps along the cable into the sunshine to recharge its built-in solar panels. Then it's time for another nice, long snooze ...

AMAZING ROBOTS

SlothBot has another mission monitoring endangered frogs in the South American rainforest.

GLOSSARY

algorithm a set of instructions that tell a computer what to do

artificial intelligence (AI) a machine that performs tasks and is programmed to think similarly to a human

disaster relief help given to the people in a place where a sudden natural disaster has occurred, such as floods or an earthquake

mimic to copy something

parallel processing when a computer divides a task into smaller parts and works on them at the same time

prosthetic an artificial body part

sensor node a small, electronic device that collects information about the environment around it

Further Reading

Books

AI in Space
by Ford Chambers (Jump! Inc, 2025)

Artificial Intelligence in the Workplace: Will AI Help Us or Hurt Us?
by Nick Hunter (Cheriton Children's Books, 2025)

Explore AI: Intelligent Robots
by Sonya Newland (Wayland, 2022)

Explore AI: Machine Learning
by Sonya Newland (Wayland, 2022)

Websites

kids.nationalgeographic.com/awesome-8/article/robots
Information about 8 really cool robots!

www.bbc.co.uk/bitesize/articles/zjfxs82
Information about what AI is and how it works

INDEX

algorithms 9
Antarctica 19
Archytas 27
art 5, 10–11
  Edmond De Belamy 11
Artificial Intelligence (AI) 4, 5, 6, 7, 8, 10, 11

batteries 15, 29
blood 12, 13
brains 7, 13, 25

chess 8–9
climate change 28, 29
computers 5, 8, 9, 13, 19, 25
  Deep Blue supercomputer 8–9
cyborgs 24–25

data 21, 29
disasters 22, 23

ecobots 14–15
electronics 7, 25
environment 5, 15, 28, 29
  extreme environments 18–19
experiments 4, 20, 21
exploration 18–19

ice 18–19

Jupiter 19
  Europa (moon) 19

lasers 16–17, 21

magnets 13
Mars 4, 17, 20–21
Mars rovers 17, 20–21
medicine 5, 9, 12–13
microchips 25
molecules 7

nanobots 12–13

oceans 19

programs/programming 5, 11
prosthetic limbs 25

rescue robots 22–23

scientists 13, 18, 19, 20, 21, 29
self-driving vehicles 17, 20, 21
self-repairing robots 4, 6–7, 18–19
sensors 7, 15, 17, 29
  LiDAR 17
SlothBot 28–29
snakes, robot 22–23
solar power 19, 29
space 10, 11, 18, 19, 20, 21
steam 27

viruses 12

Warwick, Kevin 25
waste 14, 15